6/15

Healthy Lifestyles

# DIET AND NUTRITION

Katie Dicker

amicus

mankato, minnesota

This book has been published in cooperation with Evans Publishing Group

© Evans Brothers Limited 2010
This edition published under license from Evans Brothers Limited

Published in the United States by
Amicus
P.O. Box 1329, Mankato, Minnesota 56002

Printed in China by Midas Printing International Ltd

Library of Congress Cataloging-in-Publication Data

Dicker, Katie.
  Diet and nutrition / Katie Dicker.
     p. cm. -- (Healthy lifestyles)
  Includes index.
  Summary: "Discusses the importance of having a balanced, healthy diet and a healthy body image in your teenage
  years, gives information on how the body digests various foods, and gives tips for making healthy choices to avoid
  eating disorders and obesity. "--Provided by publisher.
  ISBN 978-1-60753-085-5 (library binding)
  1. Teenagers--Nutrition. 2. Teenagers--Health and hygiene. 3. Diet. 4. Physical fitness for youth. I. Title.
  RJ235.D53 2011
  613'.0433--dc22

                          2009044219

**Consultant:** Adrian King
**Editor:** Sonya Newland
**Designer:** Graham Rich
**Picture researcher:** Sophie Schrey

**Picture Credits**
**Alamy:** 6 (Janine Wiedel Photolibrary), 12 (Bubbles Photolibrary), 19 (Bon Appetit), 29 (Science Photo Library),
32 (David Young-Wolff), 33 (Richard Sheppard), 35 (Photofusion Picture Library), 41 (Brian Harris); **Corbis:** 7
(Mark Richards), 13 (David Raymer), 25t (Najlah Feanny), 26 (Jeffrey L. Rotman), 27t (Andrew Brusso), 31l (Image
Source), 38l (Roy Morsch); **Dreamstime:** 11 (Franz Pfluegl); **Fotolia:** 20 (Corbis), 37 (Corbis); **Getty Images:** 30
(Time & Life Pictures); **iStock:** 8 (Gaffera), 9t (Aga & Miko Materne), 9b (Thomas Perkins), 15 (Juanmonino), 16
(Jaimie Duplass), 18t (Kelly Cline), 22 (Svetlana Gladkova), 23 (Asiseeit), 24–25, 27b (Dave Hughes), 28 (Peeter
Viisimaa), 34–35 (Aldo Murillo), 38r (Esemelwe), 39 (Jeanell Norvell), 40 (Josef Philipp), 42 (Jennifer Trenchard),
43 (Ericsphotography); **Science Photo Library:** 17 (Eye of Science); **Shutterstock:** 21 (Sonja Foos), 31r (Elena
Schweitzer), 36 (Radu Razvan).
Artwork by Graham Rich.

05 10
PO 1560

9 8 7 6 5 4 3 2 1

# Contents

# Introduction

Food and fluids are the fuels we need to keep on the move. Without them, our bodies can't function properly. Eating and drinking are ways of giving your body the nutrients it needs.

*It can be fun to grab a bite to eat with friends when you're out and about, but regular healthy meals are an important part of a balanced lifestyle.*

## Fuel for Life

Every time you eat, your body absorbs the nutrients from your food. It uses these nutrients to create energy, to grow new cells, and to repair and maintain old cells. When you get hungry or thirsty, it's a sign that your body needs more nutrients. Just as a car needs fuel to keep going, your body runs out of fuel if you don't eat and drink regularly. Food and fluids give you the energy you need to go about your daily tasks and help keep your body in top condition.

### ON THE RUN

*We all lead busy lives, and achieving a balanced diet when you're on the move can be difficult. Sometimes it can be tempting to grab convenience foods, such as fast food, but these foods can have a poor nutritional value. They are often high in fat, sugar, and salt.*

## Regular Meals

Your body needs a variety of foods at regular intervals to keep healthy. The type and quality of the foods you eat are important to ensure your body has all the ingredients it needs to work efficiently. But how much you eat is a factor, too. This depends on your age, your gender, your body size, and the amount of physical activity that you do.

We're all different, and the food choices that we make reflect our likes and dislikes. Some people don't like the taste or texture of particular foods. Others have an allergy to specific ingredients. Some people choose to follow a vegan or vegetarian diet, or follow strict customs about the foods they eat. Whatever your preferences, eating a balanced diet throughout life is the best way to stay healthy.

## Malnutrition

Malnutrition means "bad eating." It can be caused by eating too much or too little, or by having an unbalanced diet. In some parts of the world, food shortages and poverty mean that people are starving. This is the most extreme form of malnutrition. The body burns carbohydrates and fat to create energy (see pages 8–10) but when these run out, it begins to burn muscle tissue instead. In severe cases, this can cause muscle atrophy, organ failure, or even death. Although the world produces enough food for everyone, poverty and poor food distribution in some countries mean that almost one billion people do not have enough to eat.

## FEEL-GOOD FACTOR

*Combining a balanced diet with exercise is the best way to give your body a boost. Exercise trains your body to use your food more efficiently, so you can eat more without gaining weight. A balanced diet with regular exercise also helps to maintain a healthy immune system and makes you feel more energized.*

## Obesity

In other parts of the world, malnutrition of a different kind is causing an alarming health problem—obesity. With an abundance of food and more sedentary lifestyles, people's lives are at risk because they're eating more than they need. This can lead to serious health conditions, such as diabetes, heart disease, stroke, and some cancers.

No single food provides all the nutrients that your body needs. Instead, a balanced diet is the key to staying healthy. This means eating a variety of foods in the right proportions (see page 31). We all have different requirements, depending on our body shape, size, and our levels of activity. Learning about the way your body digests food is the first step to identifying a balanced diet that is right for you.

*Obesity is an increasing problem among young people.*

# The Body's Fuel

To get the best from our bodies, we need to eat a mixture of different types of foods at regular intervals. Nutritionists study the effects of food and offer dietary advice for optimum health.

Sugary foods such as pastries are a tasty treat, but they contain few nutrients.

## The Best Time to Start

It's important to have a balanced diet in your teen years because your body is growing and developing. If you get into the habit of a healthy diet while you're young, it will be easier to keep healthy as you grow older. Studies have also shown that overweight and underweight teenagers are more likely to experience health problems later in life, even if they start to eat healthily as an adult.

## The Five Food Groups

Nutritionists have identified five food groups that are the key to a balanced diet—carbohydrates, proteins, fats, vitamins, and minerals. Eating a balanced diet means eating the correct proportions of these five food groups, with water and fiber included.

## Carbohydrates

Our main source of energy comes from carbohydrates. Your body breaks down carbohydrates into glucose (sugar) that combines with oxygen in your cells to create energy. This process is called "cellular respiration."

There are two types of carbohydrates—simple carbohydrates (sugars) and complex carbohydrates (starches). Sugars are found in foods such as fruits and vegetables (natural sugars) or cookies, chocolate, and soft drinks (refined sugars). Starches are found in foods such as pasta, rice, and bread. You need lots of carbohydrates if your body is growing or if you're always on the move.

The body can absorb simple carbohydrates very quickly (see page 16). Simple carbohydrates give you an instant burst of energy, but the effect can soon wear off, leaving you feeling tired and hungry again. In contrast, your body has to break down complex carbohydrates before they are absorbed. This slower process keeps you feeling fuller for longer and gives you more balanced energy levels.

## REAL LIFE

"I used to crave sweet things to give me energy. I knew sugar could make you fat, but I wasn't gaining weight. My doctor told me to eat more complex carbohydrates, such as oats and pasta. Now I have more energy during the day and don't need sweet fixes to keep me going."

Sally, 16

*Carbohydrates, found in food such as pasta, give you energy.*

In a healthy meal, carbohydrates should make up about a third of what you eat, with an emphasis on starches. If you eat more carbohydrates than your body needs, they're converted to glycogen (a source of glucose) and stored in the muscles and liver until they're needed. Additional carbohydrates can also be converted to fat that is stored around the body.

## Proteins

Proteins are the nutrients your body needs to grow and repair cells and tissues. They are found in foods such as lean meat, fish, eggs, nuts, and dairy products. Grains and legumes are good sources of protein, too. Proteins are made up of molecules called amino acids. During the digestive process (see pages 14–19), the body breaks proteins down into amino acids that are carried in the blood to other parts of the body, where they reform to make new tissue such as muscle, bone, skin, and hair. Proteins are also

(see pages 14–19)

## FEEL-GOOD FACTOR

*Refined sugars are full of energy but don't contain any nutrients. Too much sugar is bad for your teeth and can lead to health conditions such as diabetes. There's lots of hidden sugar in packaged foods. Instead of soft drinks, try 100 percent fruit juice. Make your own pasta sauce instead of buying one that's ready made.*

used to make special chemicals called enzymes that help to speed up chemical reactions in the body. If you need energy for a long period of time (or are starving), proteins can also be converted to glucose to provide energy.

*Proteins help generate new tissue, building muscle and giving you strength.*

# The Body's Fuel

## Fats

Fats are another important source of energy. They are found in foods such as milk, cheese, butter, eggs, meat, and oily fish. Oils used for frying, dressings, and dips are sources of fat, too.

Fats don't dissolve in the blood like other foods (see page 16). During the digestive process, they're broken down into fatty acids or glycerol (a source of glucose). If you exercise intensely, fats can be converted to energy, but usually they're stored in fat cells under the skin and around organs such as the heart and lungs. Fats are often regarded as unhealthy, but it's important to have some fats in your diet. Stored fats are a useful source of energy if your body runs out of carbohydrates. Fats are also used to build and maintain cell walls, to protect body cells (such as nerve cells in the brain), to absorb and transport fat-soluble vitamins (A, D, E, and K, see page 11), to make substances such as hormones, and to keep the body warm.

## Types of Fats

There are two types of fats—saturated fats and unsaturated fats. Saturated fats are solid at room temperature. They are generally found in meat and dairy products, such as milk and butter. Unsaturated fats are usually liquid at room temperature. They are found in oily fish, nuts and seeds, avocados, and vegetable oils.

Fats contain a lot of energy, so eating more fat than your body needs can lead to weight gain. Eating too many saturated fats has also been linked to a higher risk of heart disease. Saturated fats contain a substance called cholesterol that, over time, can cause fatty deposits to build up in the arteries. In contrast, unsaturated fats have been found to actually lower cholesterol in the blood. They also provide essential fatty acids that the body can't make itself. Oily fish (such as sardines and salmon), for example, are good sources of omega-3 fatty acids. Some studies have shown that they help to protect the body against heart disease.

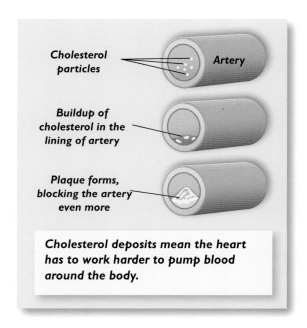

Cholesterol particles

Artery

Buildup of cholesterol in the lining of artery

Plaque forms, blocking the artery even more

**Cholesterol deposits mean the heart has to work harder to pump blood around the body.**

## A GOOD DAIRY DIET

*Dairy foods are important for healthy bones and teeth, but they can be high in fat, too. To enjoy the health benefits of dairy foods, try using skim milk, low-fat hard cheeses or cottage cheese, and low-fat yogurt instead of cream.*

## Vitamins and Minerals

Vitamins and minerals are found in fruits and vegetables. Your body needs small amounts of vitamins and minerals to help it function. These nutrients control the growth and repair of tissues and can help the body produce energy.

| VITAMIN | COMMON FOOD SOURCE | BENEFITS |
| --- | --- | --- |
| A | Liver, carrots, dairy products | Healthy eyes, skin, nails, and hair |
| B | Egg yolk, meat, yeast | Healthy nerves and digestive system |
| C | Citrus fruits, vegetables | Tissue repair and strong immune system |
| D | Fish oil, liver | Strong teeth and bones and healthy nervous system |
| E | Vegetable oils, green leafy vegetables, grains | An antioxidant that protects cell membranes. May also reduce cholesterol in the blood |
| K | Eggs, liver, green leafy vegetables | Helps the blood to clot |

| MINERAL | COMMON FOOD SOURCE | BENEFITS |
| --- | --- | --- |
| Calcium | Dairy products, green leafy vegetables | Helps to build strong teeth and bones |
| Iodine | Fish | Good for the thyroid |
| Iron | Liver, green leafy vegetables | Helps red blood cells to carry oxygen around the body |
| Selenium | Meat, fish, avocados, brazil nuts | An antioxidant that protects cell membranes |
| Magnesium | Whole grain cereals, nuts, green leafy vegetables | Healthy nerve and muscle cells |

*This table shows the source of some common vitamins and minerals, and their benefits to the body.*

Studies have shown that people who eat five portions of fruits and vegetables a day are at a lower risk of heart disease, stroke, and certain cancers. Chemicals known as antioxidants in fruits and vegetables have been found to boost the body's immune system against these diseases.

## FEEL-GOOD FACTOR

*Having five portions of fruit and vegetables a day is easier than you might think. Try a sliced banana with your breakfast cereal and a glass of fruit juice. A mid-morning orange, a side salad at lunch, and a portion of vegetables at dinner will soon get you on your way!*

*A varied diet with plenty of fresh fruits and vegetables should provide all the vitamins and minerals that you need.*

# The Body's Fuel

## Fiber

Fiber is also an important part of a balanced diet. Fiber is difficult to digest and doesn't contain any nutrients, but it helps to keep the digestive system healthy. Fiber is found in foods such as fruits, vegetables, whole grain bread, brown pasta, rice, beans, nuts, bran, and grains.

There are two types of fiber—soluble and insoluble. Insoluble fiber is fiber the body can't break down. Instead, it makes your food more bulky, helping your digestive tract to grip your food as it moves through the digestive system (see page 18). Foods that contain insoluble fiber include wholemeal bread, brown rice, wholegrain breakfast cereals, fruits, and vegetables.

Soluble fiber can be partially digested. It forms a thick gel that helps to slow down the speed at which food leaves your stomach. This keeps you feeling fuller longer so you don't eat too much. As soluble fiber passes through the intestines, it absorbs water and makes the waste softer and more bulky. This increases the ease with which food passes through the intestines, helping to avoid constipation and diseases of the digestive tract.

Soluble fiber has also been found to reduce cholesterol in the blood by binding cholesterol to waste material that is passed out of the body. Sources of soluble

*A healthy, high-fiber breakfast can set you up for the day.*

fiber include oats and legumes (such as beans and lentils).

## Water

Water is vital to keep your body functioning at its best. Water helps transport nutrients around your body and to flush out waste and harmful toxins. Many chemical reactions in your body also need water to work. Water makes up about two-thirds of the body. Every day you lose around 0.5 gallon (2 L) of water when you sweat, breathe, and go to the bathroom, but you replace this with the food and fluid that you eat and drink.

You can survive for about 60 days without solid food, but you can't survive for more than a few days without water. You'll find that you need to drink more in hot weather or after exercising. Someone who is physically overexerted in hot conditions without replacing fluids could become seriously ill in a matter of hours.

## BRAIN FOODS

*Some nutrients in food affect the brain: fatty acids help the brain develop; proteins help the brain to process things quickly; simple carbohydrates give the brain energy; and nutrients protect the brain from damage. Next time you revise your diet, think about the foods that get your gray matter working at its best!*

## Salt

Dietary guidelines often refer to the benefits of a low-salt diet. The body needs some salt to control the flow of water in and out of cells, but too much salt can raise blood pressure (which can lead to heart disease or stroke) and can cause arthritis in some people. We lose salt when we sweat, so some salt is needed to replace it.

*It's important to remain properly hydrated throughout the day, but especially after exercising, when you need to replace fluid in the body.*

The World Health Organization recommends an average salt intake of no more than 6 grams per person per day. Salt is often added to food for flavor or as a preservative, causing people to eat more salt than they need. Even if you don't add salt to your food, you may find that you're eating more than you realize in processed foods. A small bag of salted chips, for example, contains 0.5 grams of salt, but so does a bowl of cornflakes. Try to be aware of the salt content of the foods you eat.

## DID YOU KNOW?

*Brown bread and brown rice contain more fiber, vitamins, and minerals than white bread or white rice. White flour and rice are milled to remove layers of the grain's outer husk.*

# Absorbing Nutrients

Your digestive system is designed to turn your food into smaller substances that your body can absorb. This complex system works hard to get all the nutrients it can from your food.

## The Digestive Tract

The digestive system is made up of a long tube called the digestive tract. As your food passes through the digestive system, it's broken down mechanically and chemically into very small molecules that can be absorbed into the blood and taken to different parts of the body. These nutrients help to carry out essential processes, such as activating the brain, maintaining a healthy body temperature, and moving muscles. They are also used to repair damaged cells.

## Crunch Time

Your mouth is the first stage of the digestive process. Even before you eat, your digestive system gets to work. When you see or smell something good to eat,

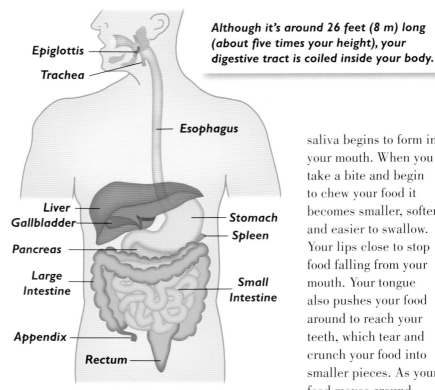

Epiglottis

Trachea

Esophagus

Liver
Gallbladder

Pancreas

Large
Intestine

Appendix

Rectum

Stomach

Spleen

Small
Intestine

*Although it's around 26 feet (8 m) long (about five times your height), your digestive tract is coiled inside your body.*

saliva begins to form in your mouth. When you take a bite and begin to chew your food it becomes smaller, softer, and easier to swallow. Your lips close to stop food falling from your mouth. Your tongue also pushes your food around to reach your teeth, which tear and crunch your food into smaller pieces. As your food moves around, it becomes coated in saliva. This contains an enzyme called amylase, which begins to break down the starch in your food into smaller molecules. As your food becomes smaller, it also has a greater surface area so more saliva can react with it.

## A HELPING HAND

*If you chew your food thoroughly and eat slowly, it puts less burden on your digestive system. With smaller pieces of food to tackle and a steady supply of ingredients, your digestive system can work more effectively.*

## Take a Gulp

When you're ready to swallow your food, it moves to the back of your throat towards the esophagus (food pipe). This stretchy tube—about 10 inches (25 cm) long and 1 inch (2.5 cm) wide—links your mouth to your stomach. Your trachea (windpipe) is at the back of your throat, too. To prevent you from choking, a special flap called the epiglottis covers the opening of the trachea when you swallow to stop food or drink from going down the wrong way.

The tubes of the digestive tract are lined with muscles that help your food to pass through them. This muscle action is called peristalsis. The tubes narrow as the muscles contract, pushing the food and liquid along—a bit like squeezing a tube of toothpaste. The lining of the digestive tract also produces digestive juices that help to break down your food.

## DID YOU KNOW?

*The action of peristalsis means that astronauts floating in space can swallow their food when they are upside down.*

At the entrance to the stomach, a ring of muscle relaxes to allow the food to pass through. Sometimes, if this muscle doesn't close tightly between meal times, acid from your stomach can enter the esophagus and cause a burning sensation. This is called heartburn (although it has nothing to do with the heart).

*When you take a bite of food, the taste buds on your tongue help you enjoy it, and alert you if any food has gone bad.*

# Absorbing Nutrients

## Food Mixer

Your stomach is like a large sack that stores the foods that you swallow. It expands when you eat and drink, and can hold about 1.6 quarts (1.5 L). The strong muscular walls of the stomach mix your food around, while the stomach lining secretes enzymes,

digestive juices, and acids that break down your food. They help to dissolve the nutrients in your food and to kill any bacteria, viruses, or parasites. Luckily, the stomach lining has a thick layer of mucus to stop the acids from wearing it away.

Some simple sugars are small enough to be absorbed into the bloodstream through the stomach wall, but the rest of your food passes to the next stage of the digestive tract. Another ring of muscle in the stomach relaxes and opens at regular intervals, allowing your half-digested food to pass to the small intestine.

## Small Intestine

The small intestine is a tube about 20 feet (6 m) long. The lining of this tube produces enzymes that break down your food, aided by digestive juices from the pancreas, liver, and gallbladder (see page 17). It is here that your body begins to absorb most of the nutrients from your food into the bloodstream. The lining of the small intestine has many tight folds, covered with tiny finger-like projections called villi. The villi are covered with even smaller projections called microvilli. These lumps and bumps greatly increase the surface area of the small intestine, allowing more and more nutrients to be absorbed. Runny food is absorbed through the villi to a network of blood vessels. The villi are just one cell thick, so food molecules pass through them very easily.

*The sugar in soft drinks passes quickly through the stomach wall and into your bloodstream.*

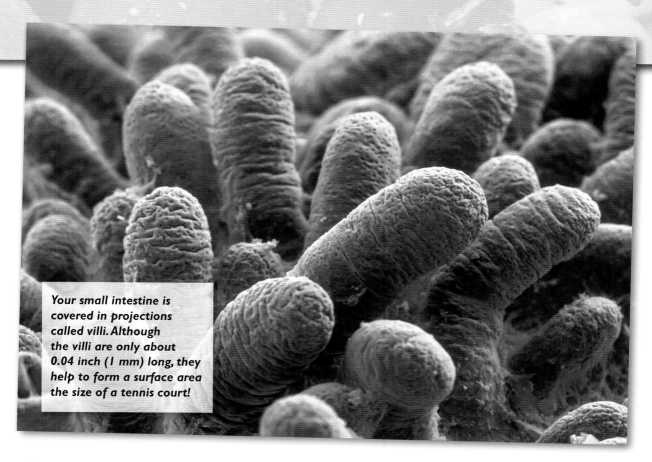

Your small intestine is covered in projections called villi. Although the villi are only about 0.04 inch (1 mm) long, they help to form a surface area the size of a tennis court!

## Liver, Gallbladder, and Pancreas

The liver, gallbladder, and pancreas are not part of the digestive tract, but they help to process and store nutrients that come from the small intestine. The liver filters nutrient-rich blood from the small intestine to remove waste material. The nutrients are then transported around the body, via the blood, to build and maintain cells or to create energy. The liver also acts as an important storehouse. It stores vital nutrients, such as iron, as well as glycogen (see page 9) until glucose is needed.

The liver also produces a digestive juice called bile. This brown-yellow liquid passes to the small intestine, where it helps to break up fats so they can be absorbed into the blood. The bile also helps neutralize some of the harmful stomach acid, enabling enzymes to work more efficiently. Extra bile is stored in the gallbladder until it is needed.

The pancreas also makes digestive juices that help to break up food in the small intestine. More importantly, however, the pancreas makes a hormone called insulin that helps body cells to use and store the glucose in food to create energy. This process controls glucose levels in the blood (see page 28).

## STOMACH STORE

*The amount of time that food spends in your stomach depends on the type of food that you eat. Simple carbohydrates, for example, spend the least amount of time and fats the longest. Some foods stay in the stomach for up to four hours.*

# Absorbing Nutrients

## Large Intestine

By the time your food passes from your small intestine to your large intestine, it has become a thin, watery mixture. Most of the nutrients from your food have been absorbed and the remainder is leftover water, dead bacteria, tiny pieces of intestine lining, and fiber that your body can't use. The large intestine is about 5 feet (1.5 m) long. Here, water and minerals, such as iron and calcium, are absorbed into the blood. Water is absorbed from your food so your body doesn't become dehydrated. As the body absorbs more water, the waste material becomes firmer—what we call feces. The feces are pushed into the rectum (see page 16), where they stay until you go to the bathroom.

out any waste products from your blood. This prevents a build-up of waste in the body that could cause damage. Blood travels to the kidneys through the renal artery. Here, the blood is filtered and waste products, such as "urea," are squeezed out. The waste moves to your bladder, where it is stored as urine until you go to the bathroom. Meanwhile, the kidneys release some water and important chemicals (such as sodium, phosphorus, and potassium) back into the blood and return it to the bloodstream through the renal vein. This helps to control the balance of substances in the body.

*It takes a hot dog seven hours to work its way through your digestive system.*

## HOW LONG DOES FOOD TAKE TO DIGEST?

| | |
|---|---|
| *Banana:* | *4 hours* |
| *Bowl of cereal:* | *4 hours* |
| *Hot dog:* | *7 hours* |
| *Red meat:* | *12 hours* |
| *Gum:* | *Never.* |

*Gum doesn't digest.*
*It eventually passes through you.*

## Kidneys

Your kidneys aren't part of the digestive tract, but their job is to filter the blood. These two bean-shaped organs are each about the size of a fist. When your body has taken all the nutrients it needs from your food, the kidneys filter

### How the Kidney Works

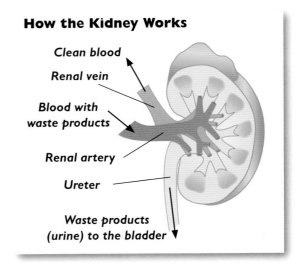

Clean blood

Renal vein

Blood with waste products

Renal artery

Ureter

Waste products (urine) to the bladder

*Every day, your kidneys process about 53 gallons (200 L) of blood and filter out about 1/2 gallon (2 L) of excess water and waste products.*

## Good and Bad Bacteria

There are thought to be 500–100,000 different types of bacteria living in the digestive tract. We usually think of bacteria as dangerous. Although some bacteria in your digestive system can cause harm, most of the time they live in balance with good bacteria that are really useful to your body. Good bacteria (probiotics) help boost your immune system and prevent allergies. They also help to overpower bacteria (such as E. coli and salmonella) that cause food poisoning. The bacteria in your digestive system help to break your food down as it passes through the digestive tract. They also help produce enzymes that speed up the digestive process. Studies have shown that without them, we'd have to eat about 30 percent more calories to maintain a healthy body weight.

Eating a varied diet will keep a healthy balance of good and bad bacteria in your digestive system. When this balance is upset, however, it can make you ill. Eating too much sugar, for example, can feed the bad bacteria that cause disease, overpowering the good

bacteria that keep you healthy. This can lead to bacterial infections such as thrush (or candida). Similarly, if you have antibiotics because you are ill, the medication can affect the good bacteria in addition to the bad bacteria it's trying to target. Adding probiotic foods to your diet, such as yogurt, can help increase the amount of good bacteria to restore balance to your digestive system.

*Some yogurts and other products now contain good bacteria to help keep your intestines healthy.*

# The Right Amount

In the Western world, with so much food at our disposal, we're spoiled with choice. We're also in danger of overeating. So just how much food do we really need?

### Changing Times

Today, we have a more varied diet than ever before. Our grocery stores are full of food and prices have become cheaper, with new farming techniques increasing food production and improved transport links importing and exporting goods around the world.

But our lifestyles are changing, too. With technology developing at an unprecedented rate, our lives have become easier. In theory we have more time—we no longer have to hunt for our food or search for shelter—but our lifestyles are moving at a faster pace. Instead of savoring our meals, fast food has become a convenient way to eat while doing all the other things we enjoy. We've developed a taste for foods that are high in sugar and fat, and decreasing levels of physical activity mean we're not balancing our food intake effectively. Our use of cars, TV remote controls, and other machinery means we're less active than ever before. Food portions have also increased. King-size candy bars, giant bags of chips, and large plates of food encourage us to eat more.

### How Much Is Enough?

How much you need to eat depends on your age, your gender, and your body size. If you are tall and have a big build, your body has more cells to grow and maintain. Men tend to need more food than women because they have more muscle tissue in their body—muscle burns more energy than any other body tissue. The amount of physical activity that you do is

*Ordering take-out food has become part of our everyday lives, but this food is often high in fat and not nutritionally balanced.*

## DID YOU KNOW?

*Researchers in the United States have discovered that over thousands of years, changes in our diet have influenced our genes. Most people, for example, can digest milk in adulthood (whereas most animals only drink milk in infancy). This trait became apparent when early Europeans tamed cows, and milk became a major part of their diet.*

also an important factor. When you exercise, you increase the amount of oxygen in your blood and burn more energy. The more energy you burn, the less that is stored as fat.

## Food Through Life

You need to change the amount of food that you eat at different times of your life. Growing children, pregnant women, and training athletes, for example, need more food to help their bodies cope with changes and extra demands. In contrast, elderly people need less food because they are less active and their muscles become slightly smaller.

During your teens, your bones grow a lot, so calcium is important. Studies have shown that around half of bone mass is formed during the teenage years. Calcium is also important to prevent bone diseases, such as osteoporosis, later in life. Boys tend to grow more than girls during their teen years, so they need to take in more protein and energy to cope with this growth spurt. Iron is also important for healthy growth and the development of muscles. Iron is particularly important for girls when they reach puberty, because some iron is lost during menstruation.

## GROWING PAINS

*The teenage growth spurt begins at around 10 years of age (in girls) and 12 (in boys). During your teen years, you will grow in height by an average of 9 inches (23 cm) and in weight by about 44–57 lbs (20–26 kg). As a child, you typically have about 15 percent body fat. During your teen years, this increases to about 20 percent in girls, and decreases to about 10 percent in boys.*

*You'll go through a growth spurt in your teens, so eating properly is important to keep your bones and muscles strong.*

# The Right Amount

## Calories

One way of measuring how much energy our food contains is to count calories. Most food labels advertise the number of calories in a particular product. In scientific terms, a calorie is the amount of energy needed to raise the temperature of one kilogram of water by one degree Celsius. You use calories for energy when you exercise, but your body also uses them for everyday functions such as keeping your heart beating, your lungs working, and your brain active. Your brain, liver, and muscles use the most energy—they each use about a fifth of the energy you need when you are resting.

## Burning Energy

When you get active, you burn more calories. The rate at which you burn energy varies from person to person, but the following table acts as a guide of relative use.

| ACTIVITY | CALORIES PER HOUR* |
|---|---|
| Stretching | 180 |
| Bicycling (<10 mph) | 290 |
| Hiking | 370 |
| Basketball | 440 |
| Aerobics | 480 |

\* for a 154 lb. (70 kg) person

### CALORIE COUNTING

*Researchers have found that archaea (a microbe in the digestive tract) helps bacteria to digest particular sugars, increasing the number of calories absorbed. Archaea is thought to be present in 50 to 85 percent of humans. This confirms the view that diets affect individuals in different ways—it's less about how many calories are in food and more about how many calories your body absorbs.*

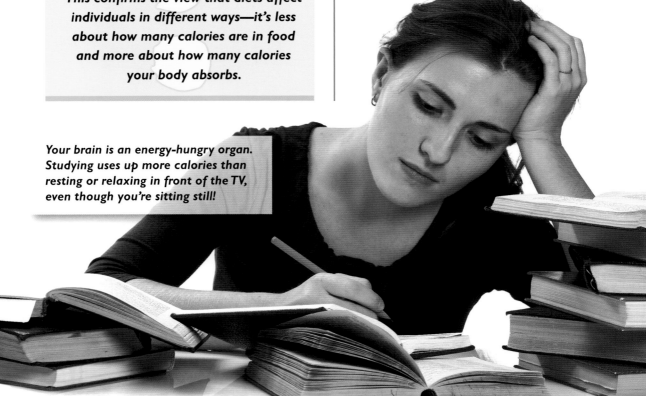

*Your brain is an energy-hungry organ. Studying uses up more calories than resting or relaxing in front of the TV, even though you're sitting still!*

## Metabolism

Metabolism is the process by which your body uses energy from food. The speed at which your body uses this energy is called your metabolic rate. We all have different metabolisms. If you have a fast metabolism, you use calories quickly so you can probably eat more without gaining weight. If you have a slow metabolism, your body burns food more slowly and you may find you gain weight easily.

There are three types of metabolism—resting metabolism, digestion metabolism, and active metabolism. Resting metabolism is sometimes called your basal metabolic rate (BMR). This is the rate at which your body burns energy to maintain basic functions, such as breathing, circulating blood, and keeping warm—these activities occur even when you are resting or asleep. Active metabolism is the rate at which your body burns energy for movement, and digestion metabolism is the rate at which your body burns energy when it absorbs the nutrients from your food.

If you lead an active lifestyle, you are likely to have a higher metabolic rate, which burns more calories.

## DID YOU KNOW?

*You generate heat when your body burns calories. This is why you feel warm after eating. The energy from food helps to keep your body at a regular temperature.*

## Changing Metabolic Rate

Your BMR varies throughout the day and changes as you get older. If you have a large body shape, you'll have a higher BMR than someone smaller because you need more calories each day to maintain your cells and your body works harder to digest additional food. In your teenage years, your BMR increases to aid growth and development. As you get older, your BMR decreases because you are less active and your muscles shrink.

Men tend to have a higher BMR because they have more muscle tissue in their body—muscle burns 90 percent more calories than fat. Exercise can increase BMR because it helps to develop muscles. Larger, stronger muscles also mean you store more energy. Your BMR can increase for up to two days after exercise, and regular exercise can increase it permanently. A higher metabolic rate is good for maintaining a healthy weight, but it also helps your body to release energy, giving you extra vitality.

# The Right Amount

### Different Shapes and Sizes

Scientists have identified three main body types —endomorph, ectomorph, and mesomorph. They believe this variation has helped the human species to survive—heavier people with stored fat are more likely to survive a famine, for example, while leaner people are more likely to be able to run quickly from danger. We all come in different shapes and sizes, and it can be useful to recognize your body type to learn more about how your metabolism works for you.

### Body Mass Index

The most common way of gauging how much body fat someone has is to use the body mass index (BMI). To calculate your BMI:

1. *Weigh yourself in pounds*
2. *Measure your height in inches.*
3. *Divide your weight in pounds by your height squared. Take that number and multiply it by 703:*

$$\frac{weight\ in\ pounds}{(height\ in\ inches)^2} \times 703 = BMI$$

*A BMI below 18.5 is underweight, 20 to 25 is a healthy weight and over 30 is obese.*

Measuring BMI helps to identify the risk of different health conditions. Scientists have found that people with a BMI over 25, for example, have an increased risk of suffering from serious diseases such as heart disease, diabetes, high blood pressure, stroke, and some types of cancer (such as breast cancer).

Although BMI is a good indication of fat levels, it isn't an accurate measure in all cases. Athletes, for example, have more lean muscle on their body. This means that they can have a high BMI without being overweight. The BMI was designed for healthy adults, so it isn't accurate for children, young people, or older adults. Instead, specific age-adjusted charts are used.

*Whatever your body shape, combining a balanced diet with regular exercise is the best way to keep in top condition.*

Doctors usually take other factors into consideration when assessing whether someone is overweight. These include blood pressure, blood cholesterol, blood sugar, and waist size. Studies have shown that fat around the stomach rather than around the hips and thighs, for example, can lead to health problems such as heart disease and diabetes.

*Rising levels of childhood obesity are causing concern among experts. Poor eating habits in childhood usually continue into adulthood.*

## A Growing Problem

Studies have shown that levels of obesity are growing at an alarming rate.

In the United States, obesity levels have more than doubled since 1960 among adults, with most of the rise occurring since 1980. Nearly a third of U.S. adults are currently obese. And a similar trend has affected American children and teenagers. In 2003, for example,

35 percent of boys and 26 percent of girls (ages 10 to 17) from the United States were obese. In 2004, researchers predicted that obesity would soon pass tobacco-related diseases as the leading cause of preventable death. Statistics are similar in Canada. In 2004, 23.1% of Canadians 18 years of age or older were classified as obese.

In contrast, a national health survey done in 1978–79 showed only 18% of adult Canadians classified as obese.

The United States and Canada are not the only countries affected. With global adult obesity levels currently at over 300 million, the World Health Organization estimates that there will be over 700 million obese adults in the world by 2015.

## A GROWING NATION

**In the past 30 years, the height of the average 20-year-old Japanese male has increased by 4 inches (10 cm) and the average female by nearly 2.8 inches (7 cm.) The cause is thought to be a change in diet—the consumption of grains has declined and meat and dairy products have increased.**

| BODY TYPE | | |
| --- | --- | --- |
| **ENDOMORPH** | **MESOMORPH** | **ECTOMORPH** |
| • naturally wide, round, and curvy<br>• "apple" or "pear" shaped<br>• slow metabolism<br>• more fat cells so easier to gain weight and more difficult to lose it | • naturally athletic<br>• hourglass shape (females) or triangular/rectangular shape (males)<br>• moderate metabolism<br>• develop lean muscle easily and find it easy to lose weight (but lack of exercise or an unbalanced diet can cause weight gain) | • naturally slim<br>• long or rectangular body shape<br>• naturally high metabolism<br>• difficult to gain weight (as either fat or lean muscle)<br>• healthy diet and regular exercise still important to keep in top condition |

# You Are What You Eat

When our bodies absorb the food that we eat, the nutrients help to carry out vital processes. That's why the type, quality, and quantity of our food is so important.

## Undereating

If you don't eat enough—or enough of the right types of food—your body is deprived of vital nutrients. You may feel faint, tired, and cold, or your body may not develop properly. Your immune system may weaken, making you more prone to coughs and colds. You may feel that you have less energy or that you feel down and depressed. In contrast, a balanced diet gives your body all the nutrients that it needs to stay healthy.

## Deficiency Diseases

Deficiency diseases are caused by a lack of nutrients. They are particularly prevalent in developing countries, where food shortages lead to severe malnutrition. However, an unbalanced diet, or an inability to absorb nutrients effectively, can lead to deficiencies, too. Vitamin deficiencies cause diseases such as anemia, scurvy, osteoporosis, and rickets. Anemia occurs when the body doesn't have enough red blood cells to transport oxygen around it. The disease can be caused by a diet lacking in iron and vitamin B. In many countries, iron compounds are now added to foods, such as flour and grain, to help prevent anemia.

*Rickets is a disease caused by a lack of vitamin D. It causes the bones in the legs to bend because they cannot support the weight of the body.*

## COMFORT FOODS

*Scientists think they know why some comfort foods, such as cookies and candy, are more appealing in times of stress. These foods, which are high in fat and carbohydrates, help to suppress stress hormones. However, in the long-term, they can actually increase stress hormones and lead to weight gain.*

**Super Size Me** *was a social commentary on the dangers of the fast-food society in which we now live.*

Osteoporosis is a condition that causes bones to become weak and prone to fractures. A diet with good levels of calcium and vitamin D can help to reduce the risk of osteoporosis. Rickets is a disease caused by a severe vitamin D deficiency, resulting in soft bones that cannot support the weight of a growing body. Fish, liver, and exposure to sunlight can help to reduce the risk of rickets.

Scurvy is caused by a lack of vitamin C and results in weakness, bleeding gums, and sores on the skin. Years ago, scurvy was particularly common in winter, when fresh fruits and vegetables were not available in many parts of the world.

### Foods of the Future

Scientists think they could help relieve the malnutrition crisis in developing countries by removing poisons from cottonseed to make it edible. This could provide food for half a billion people every year. More than 80 countries around the world grow cotton, but for every 2.2 pounds (1 kg) of fiber the plant produces, it also yields about 3.6

pounds (1.65 kg) of seed full of protein. Cottonseed is naturally poisonous to protect it from insects, but scientists have genetically modified the crop to remove these toxins. The safety of their findings will need thorough testing before cottonseed becomes a staple food, but the results give hope for countries with critical food shortages.

*Some scientists think that cotton harvests may help to address the problem of malnutrition in developing countries.*

# You Are What You Eat

## Diabetes

Another disease that can be caused by a poor diet is diabetes. Diabetes occurs when there is too much glucose in the blood. Initial symptoms include frequent urination, excessive thirst, unusual weight loss, and blurred vision.

The pancreas releases a hormone called insulin, which helps to control blood glucose levels (see page 17). Glucose comes from the carbohydrates we eat and drink, and is also stored in muscles and the liver (see page 9). When you eat carbohydrates, your blood glucose levels rise. In response, your pancreas releases insulin that helps the glucose to pass from your blood to your cells to produce energy. When the glucose has been used, levels in the blood begin to drop. To get more energy, the body uses stored glucose from the muscles and liver, or glucose from additional food, signaling the pancreas to release insulin again.

The body works best when blood glucose levels are stable. A good balance is

People from Africa, South Asia, the Caribbean, and the Middle East are up to five times more likely to have Type II diabetes than those of white origin. In this group, the disease can occur from about 25 years of age.

usually maintained by insulin moving glucose to your body's cells and glucose being replaced by the food you eat or extra stores. In some people, however, this system doesn't work properly and they develop diabetes.

## Type I and Type II

There are two types of diabetes—Type I and Type II. Type I diabetes occurs when the body is unable to produce any insulin at all. It is sometimes called "juvenile diabetes" because it often appears before the age of 40. It's a less common form of the disease but is the main cause of diabetes in childhood. Type II diabetes occurs when the body can produce insulin—but not enough, or it doesn't use the insulin it makes effectively. You're more likely to get Type II diabetes as an adult if someone in your immediate family has it, or if you're overweight. In recent years, however, obesity levels have caused a rise in Type II diabetes in children.

## A RISING TREND

An estimated 246 million people worldwide are affected by diabetes. In the United States, 23.6 million people (7.8 percent of the population) have diabetes—with rates rising rapidly. A report in 2003 claimed that nearly a third of Americans born in 2000 could develop diabetes if trends continue. Fast-developing nations, such as India and China, are also seeing extreme rises in the number of children with Type II diabetes.

## The Symptoms of Diabetes

With Type I diabetes, a lack of insulin means that glucose can't pass to the cells and levels of blood glucose rise. The body tries to filter the extra glucose through the kidneys (causing frequent urination and thirst). The body isn't able to create energy from the glucose in your food, so you feel tired. As an alternative energy source, the body begins to burn fat, which can cause weight loss. Other symptoms include blurred vision and a slow healing of wounds. This type of diabetes is treated with lifelong insulin injections.

Type II diabetes can occur in people of a healthy weight, but is becoming increasingly common in the overweight population. A build-up of fat around body cells can cause them to become resistant to insulin. With plenty of fuel around, the cells ignore signals to take in glucose from the blood and over time, they can become permanently resistant to the effects of insulin. Because the cells are still in need of energy, however, they send signals to the liver to release stored glucose. The pancreas eventually wears out with all the insulin it needs to produce to

*Some people with diabetes need insulin injections. Not everyone who gets Type II diabetes is overweight, but it is becoming increasingly common in obese people.*

keep up with rising glucose levels. Symptoms of Type II diabetes can appear very slowly—some people live with the disease for up to ten years before they are diagnosed. Treatment includes exercise and dietary changes to aid weight loss, medication, and sometimes regular insulin injections.

Most people with diabetes can manage their condition effectively to lead a healthy, active life. But in severe cases, the disease can lead to kidney failure, coma, and even death. The best way to avoid diabetes and obesity is to exercise regularly and to eat a healthy diet.

## DID YOU KNOW?

*Scientists have discovered that bones secrete a chemical that signals the pancreas to make more insulin, and encourages the body's cells to become more sensitive to insulin. Their findings could contribute toward the treatment of diabetes in people who have become insulin-resistant.*

# You Are What You Eat

## Dieting

It's important that your body receives the nutrients it needs when you're growing—you don't need to lose weight unless your body has too much fat that could put a strain on your heart. In recent years, however, the search for the ultimate body size has led to diets becoming a big business. Nutritionists are constantly debating the best way to maintain a healthy body weight—what we've learned is that a balanced diet is key. Crash diets, when you deprive your body of food or essential nutrients, can be dangerous. These diets can help you to lose weight initially, but the weight lost is usually water weight. Crash diets can actually cause your muscles to shrink, meaning that you burn less energy and gain fat more easily. Crash diets also cause what is known as the "yo-yo" effect. When your body is deprived of nutrients, it begins to store fat because it thinks food is scarce. When you return to your normal eating habits, you gain weight more easily.

*Dr. Atkins shows the food that can be eaten under his diet plan—note no carbohydrates!*

## The Great Nutrition Debate

In 2000, the U.S. government sponsored the Great Nutrition Debate—inviting top dieticians to debate their theories about the best and healthiest ways to maintain a healthy body weight.

### FEEL-GOOD FACTOR

*Diets where you only eat certain types of food can leave you short of nutrients. The best way to keep healthy is to maintain a balanced diet in the long term. It's also easier to change and maintain good eating habits over a long period of time— and the benefits are huge.*

At one extreme, the late Dr. Atkins advocated a high-protein, low-carbohydrate diet, while on the other, Dr. Ornish encouraged a diet low in fat and high in fruits and vegetables.

Atkins said that obesity was caused by fat produced by the body, not fat that the body consumed. He claimed that a low-carbohydrate diet would cause less glucose to be converted to fat. With a lack of carbohydrates, he believed the body would burn stored fat, leading to weight loss. However, critics claimed his diet contained too much saturated fat and too little fruits and vegetables, increasing the risk of heart disease and some kinds of cancer. In contrast, Dr. Ornish's low-fat diet was designed to prevent heart disease. However, critics claimed it was too strict and said people were unlikely to stick with it for very long.

## Fat Cells

Whatever diet fads arise next, scientists have discovered one significant factor about weight gain—that adults actually retain the same number of fat cells throughout life, regardless of how heavy they are. These fat cells can expand and shrink dramatically with weight gain and weight loss. This may explain why many people put on weight easily after a crash diet—the fat cells signal an energy imbalance and encourage weight gain. Instead, the best way to lose weight is to maintain healthy eating habits in the long term, to encourage your cells to store less fat.

*Even when you diet, your body retains the same number of fat cells—they just expand and shrink as you gain or lose weight.*

## Government Guidelines

Many governments produce guidelines to help people maintain a healthy weight. In 2005, for example, the U.S. Department of Agriculture (USDA) introduced "MyPyramid" to try to curb the growing problem of obesity (www.mypyramid.gov). This guidance takes account of age, gender, and exercise levels for a balanced diet.

*Well-balanced portions are key to good health, as shown here on the UK Food Standard Agency's "Eatwell Plate."*

## REAL LIFE

*"I used to smoke. I knew smoking was bad for me, but I didn't realize I was also depriving my body of important nutrients."*

*Kirsty, 19*

# Body Image

We come in all shapes and sizes, but in today's world of fad diets and celebrity culture, it's natural to wonder whether we're too fat, too thin, or just plain not good enough!

### Cultural Views

We all have different builds and weigh different amounts. Men and women also differ in their natural weights because of the varying proportion of muscle and fat in their bodies. Muscle burns more energy than fat, but it also weighs more than fat.

Fashions, culture, and prejudice can lead us to favor one body type over another. Years ago, people valued body fat because it was seen as a sign of prosperity. Fat was also seen as protection against potentially leaner times to come. This is still true in some developing

## APPETITE CONTROL

*Scientists believe that a hormone, called leptin, influences the brain and could determine whether someone is likely to be slender or obese. Fat cells produce and secrete leptin, which sends signals to the brain to suppress appetite, preventing too much weight gain. But scientists think that if leptin is restricted during early brain development (because of a genetic defect or nutritional deficiencies, for example) it could have a lasting effect on a person's ability to control body weight.*

*It is common, especially among teenagers, to feel overweight, when in fact they have perfectly healthy body shapes.*

countries, where obesity is associated with wealth and good nutrition. In rich countries, however, obesity is often regarded as a sign of poverty and malnutrition. This is because high-fat foods tend to be cheaper than healthier alternatives, attracting the less well-off.

## Personal Perceptions

While societies view weight gain and weight loss in different ways, personal perceptions can also vary. Scientists have found that teenagers' perceptions of their own body image, for example, can change according to their race, their ethnicity, and their gender. Research studies have shown that black and white teens see their bodies differently, as do boys and girls. Of girls who thought they were too fat, for example, 52 percent actually had a normal body mass index. White girls were more likely to consider themselves overweight than black girls, black boys, or white boys. Girls were also more than twice as likely as boys to want to weigh less. Boys tended to want to weigh more.

*In some cases, obesity is a genetic problem, and families often have similar body shapes.*

## All in the Genes?

For most people, diet and exercise are the key factors to maintaining a healthy body weight. In rich countries, people who are overweight are usually associated with a poor diet and low levels of physical activity. But scientists believe that, in some cases, obesity can be caused by genetic factors. When food was scarce, some of our ancestors were able to store energy as fat and this gene was passed on to their offspring. Today, we have a more secure food supply, which means that people are continuing to store fat that they don't need.

In recent years, scientists have discovered the exact genes that play a role in our metabolism. Studies have shown that a gene called adipose, for example, tells the body when to store fat and when to burn it. But despite these advances, it's still not clear why some people don't manage to maintain a natural balance between the food they eat and the energy they use. Understanding more about the genetic causes of obesity could lead to new options for treatment and prevention. In the meantime, however, nutritional balance and regular exercise continue to be the best ways of achieving a healthy body weight.

## DID YOU KNOW?

*Obesity is more prevalent within social groups. A study revealed that a person's risk of becoming obese increased by 40 percent if a sibling was overweight, or by 57 percent if a close friend was overweight (71 percent if the friend was of the same sex).*

# Body Image

## Eating Disorders

Sometimes an obsession with body image can go too far. Some people who are anxious to lose weight develop a condition called anorexia. They diet intensely in the hope of attaining an unrealistic body shape. The desire to lose weight can be overpowering and people with anorexia go to all kinds of lengths to achieve their goal. They may skip meals, exercise excessively, make themselves sick after eating, or even use laxatives so the body quickly uses any food they've eaten.

People with anorexia become very thin, sometimes losing more than 30 percent of their body weight. A BMI less than 16 can put their

### TEEN TROUBLE

*Anorexia affects around 1 in 150 15-year-old females, and 1 in 1,000 15-year-old males. About 40 percent of people with anorexia recover, while around 30 percent continue to experience the illness long-term.*

health in serious danger. Anorexia is most common in women ages 15 to 25, and is particularly common in body-image professions, such as modeling or sports.

Another related eating disorder is bulimia. People with bulimia often eat a large quantity of food in a short period of time, even if they're not hungry. They then feel guilty about the extra calories they've consumed and try to purge their bodies of the food they've eaten—they may vomit, exercise intensely, or use laxatives to lose weight. Eating disorders may start as an experimental behavior, but can develop into a psychological condition that requires therapy to treat.

## Health Impact

Depriving your body of essential nutrients can lead to a number of health problems. Extreme weight loss can cause feelings of tiredness and depression. People with anorexia often feel faint and cold. Their muscles grow smaller as their body begins to burn muscle tissue for energy. With a loss of insulating fat tissue, the body can sometimes form a layer of downy hair for warmth.

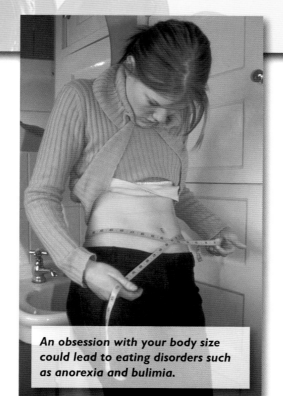

*An obsession with your body size could lead to eating disorders such as anorexia and bulimia.*

A weakened immune system also makes the body more prone to infection. Dramatic weight loss can disrupt a woman's menstrual cycle, which may affect her fertility. A change in the body's chemical balance can lead to osteoporosis, slow or stunted growth, deficiency diseases, and even heart failure.

Bulimia can lead to tooth decay because of the stomach acids induced during vomiting. Bulimia can also cause dehydration, weakness, and severe cramps. If you think that you or someone you know is suffering from an eating disorder, talk to an adult you trust. Dealing with an eating disorder can take some time, but there are support networks available that can help those affected to overcome their difficulties.

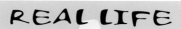

## REAL LIFE

*"I had anorexia for three years. I became fixated with food and ways to stay slim. I still don't feel 'comfortable' around food. But I've realized that my health is too important to lose."*

*Steph, 16*

*Your natural weight and body shape are what make you who you are—be proud of your physique!*

# Food Awareness

One way to begin a healthier lifestyle is to have an interest in the food you eat at home and at school. Food awareness now will teach you important skills for later in life.

## Food Shopping

Next time you help to buy groceries, think about the foods you're buying. Look at food labels to identify what nutrients they contain. With governments becoming more aware of the importance of a balanced diet, food labeling has become a common requirement. Food labels show ingredients (listed in descending order of weight), nutritional values, weight or volume, a "best before" date, and details of the food's origin.

## What to Look For

The best foods to eat are fresh foods. When food is canned or frozen, some of the vitamins and minerals are destroyed. Processed foods can also contain high levels of salt and sugar. Sometimes, chemicals called additives are put in processed foods to preserve them.

The best foods to eat are fresh foods. You can shop at the supermarket, but often farmers' markets offer fresher—and organic—foods.

Additives are also added to some foods to make them look and taste good. Many additives are harmless, but some can cause allergies (see page 39). Try to choose foods that are low in fat, salt, and sugar. Remember, too, that different nutrients contain different amounts of energy. A gram of carbohydrate and a gram of protein, for example, contain 3.75 and 4 calories, respectively. In contrast, a gram of fat contains 9 calories—over twice as much energy.

## Organic Food

When some foods are produced, farmers use artificial fertilizers or pesticides to increase the crops they yield. Animals raised for meat are also given antibiotics to keep them healthy. In contrast, organic foods are produced with strict limits on the amount of

## REAL LIFE

"Mom and Dad work during the week so I sometimes help with the shopping on my way home from school. On Tuesdays I have soccer practice so I don't get home in time for supper. I have a big lunch instead and a snack when I get home."

James, 14

Learning to cook as a teenager will teach you great skills for when you move away from home.

artificial chemicals that are used. Some people choose to buy organic food because studies have suggested they have a higher nutritional value and fewer poisons. Organic farming also has less impact on the environment. At the moment, however, organic foods are more expensive to buy because of the costs incurred in their production.

## Cooking

If you don't already help with the cooking at home, give it a try! If you become a good cook, you'll also be able to invite friends and family over for a meal. Experiment with different types of food and think about your ingredients. Storing and cooking methods change the nutritional value of the foods you eat. It's better to eat fresh fruits and vegetables as soon as possible, for example, rather than storing them for long periods of time. Fruits and vegetables should be washed, but soaking and boiling can wash out vitamins and minerals. A healthier alternative is to steam vegetables to retain their

nutrients and flavor. If you boil vegetables, you could consider using the water for a sauce or a soup to recapture some of the lost nutrients. Covering the saucepan to keep in the steam also helps to retain nutrients by speeding up the cooking time.

Try not to add too much fat to your food. Grill, bake, steam, or boil instead of roasting and frying. Try to flavor your food with herbs and spices instead of salt.

## FEEL-GOOD FACTOR

Do you skip breakfast in the rush to get up and dressed and ready for school? Breakfast is one of the most important meals of the day—it helps to balance energy levels for the day ahead, and kick-starts your metabolism. Try to make breakfast part of your daily routine.

# Food Awareness

Use clean plates and cutlery and change dishcloths regularly.

## Food Safety

The food you eat keeps your body healthy, but if germs enter your digestive system, they can make you ill. You should always wash your hands before touching food, cooking food, or eating a meal, as well as after using the bathroom. Dry your hands thoroughly, too—germs spread more easily on damp hands.

Cooking equipment needs to be kept clean, as well. Countertops, cutting boards, and utensils should be washed thoroughly. Use clean plates and cutlery and change dishcloths regularly.

## Storing, Preparing, and Reheating

It's important to keep food covered to protect it from germs in the air and from insects, such as flies. Most germs are kept at bay by storing food in cool places and cooking at high temperatures,

but certain precautions are needed. Raw meat, for example, can harbor germs and should be kept in separate, sealed containers. When cutting raw meat, wash the knife and cutting board thoroughly before you prepare other foods.

Store foods in a fridge, or preserve them in a freezer, and check "best before" dates before using. Wait for food to cool before refrigerating and eat leftovers within a couple of days. Luckily, our senses of smell and taste usually tell us when food has gone bad, but use common sense, too.

Cool conditions stop germs from multiplying —if food isn't stored in a fridge, for example, 10 germs can multiply to 1,000 germs in just six hours.

When cooking food, follow the instructions and make sure your food is hot all the way through. When reheating, check that food is throughly heated and avoid reheating or freezing more than once.

Extra care should be taken when storing and reheating rice. Uncooked rice contains spores of bacteria that can cause food poisoning. If cooked rice is left at room temperature, these bacteria can multiply and are not destroyed by reheating. Try to serve rice when it's just been cooked, or cool within an hour, and keep in the fridge before serving cold or reheating.

## Food Allergies

Some people are allergic to particular foods, such as nuts, wheat, dairy products, and additives. Food allergies are caused by an abnormal response of the immune system.

Your body's immune system produces antibodies that fight off bacteria and viruses to protect you from disease. If you are allergic to an ingredient in food, however, your body thinks you've eaten something harmful and chemicals called histamines rush to your defense. This can cause symptoms such as sickness, stomach pains, and skin rashes. A severe allergic reaction can also cause swelling of the lips, tongue, and throat, making breathing very difficult. Someone with a severe food allergy needs to carry medication with them at all times, while avoiding contact with the ingredient they're allergic to. Food labels are now required to give warnings about the presence of potential allergens in their ingredients, such as nuts or wheat.

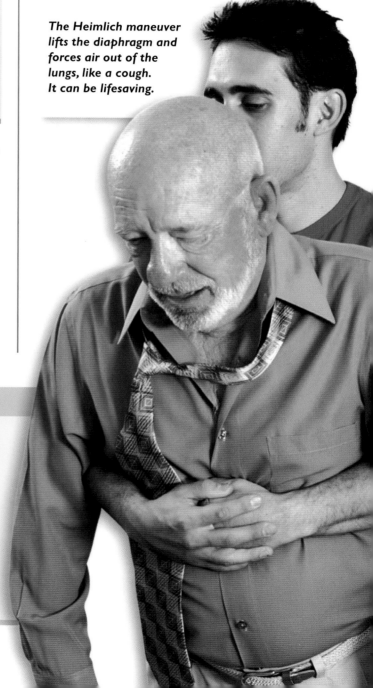

*The Heimlich maneuver lifts the diaphragm and forces air out of the lungs, like a cough. It can be lifesaving.*

## THE HEIMLICH MANEUVER

*Sometimes, food can go down the wrong way, blocking the windpipe and causing a person to choke. Cutting food into smaller pieces and chewing thoroughly can help to prevent this. If choking occurs, a series of abdominal thrusts called the Heimlich maneuver can help to dislodge the food.*

# Food for Life

Food is one of life's greatest pleasures. Mealtimes are a perfect opportunity to spend time with family and friends, and cooking is a hobby that can last a lifetime.

*A cooking class is a great way to learn more cooking skills and to meet new people.*

## Food for Fun

Use your knowledge about food to experiment with different tastes and flavors. Try new foods and think about all the nutrients they contain. Foods that are high in fat or sugar should form only a small part of your diet. It doesn't hurt to eat cookies, sweets, or chips occasionally—allow yourself treats without feeling guilty, but try to balance the foods you eat over a day or a week, for example. Try your hand at cooking, too. You could even join a cooking class to give you confidence in your cooking skills.

## Regular Routine

Try to eat moderate amounts at regular intervals —large portions will put too much stress on your digestive system. Take time to eat as well.

It's better to eat slowly, to chew each mouthful, and to take time to rest after a meal. Try not to skip meals. If you get too hungry, you may be tempted to overeat. Your digestive system will work better if it gets used to regular meals.

## TEST YOURSELF

*Keep a diary of all the foods you eat for a week, and research all the nutrients they contain. Which nutrients are you lacking from your diet? What proportions of foods are you eating? How could you help to address this balance?*

### Vegetarians and Vegans

To keep your body in top condition, your diet should contain all the nutrients you need. Some people prefer to follow a vegetarian or vegan diet. This may be because of personal preferences, cultural practices, or for ethical reasons. As with all healthy diets, balance is the key. If you're vegetarian or vegan, you may find that some nutrients (such as protein and iron) are lacking in your meat-free diet. However, there are plenty of alternative foods you could try.

Protein can be found in legumes (lentils and beans), nuts and seeds, soy, and eggs and dairy products (for non-vegans). Iron can be found in legumes, green leafy vegetables, and bread. If you're a vegan, it can be difficult to get enough vitamin B12, which usually comes from meat and dairy products. Good alternative sources are yeast extract and fortified bread or breakfast cereal. All these foods are tasty—you don't have to be vegetarian or vegan to enjoy them!

*Eating too quickly, or while you're on the move, doesn't give your body a chance to properly digest your food.*

### Eating Out

Eating out is a treat and often a way to sample your favorite foods or to try new dishes. Enjoy eating at restaurants but be aware of the foods you're eating, too. In the United States, a government campaign has led to some restaurants voluntarily listing their nutritional information, to help people maintain healthy eating habits.

# Food for Life

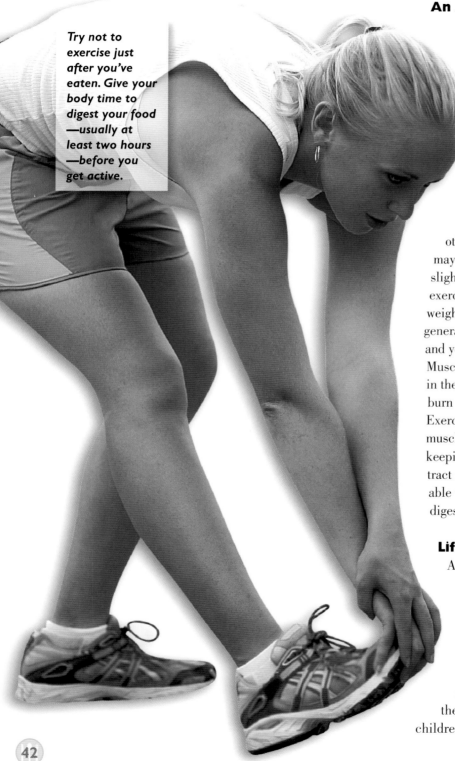

Try not to exercise just after you've eaten. Give your body time to digest your food —usually at least two hours —before you get active.

## An Active Life

Combining a balanced diet with an active life is one of the best ways to stay fit and healthy. Exercise helps to control your body weight by balancing the energy from the food you eat with the energy you use during physical activity. When you exercise, you burn energy that would otherwise be stored as fat. You may find that you gain weight slightly if you take up regular exercise. This is because muscle weighs more than fat—but your general health will improve greatly, and your body will become firmer. Muscle also burns a lot of energy, so in the long term, this will help you to burn fat that your body doesn't need. Exercise can also help to strengthen muscles around your abdomen, keeping the muscles of the digestive tract in good shape and better able to push food through your digestive system.

## Life Changes

As you go through life, remember that your diet may need to change to take account of different circumstances. Talk to your doctor if you're worried about your weight and follow recommended guidelines. In the United states, for example, children over six years of age, teenage girls, and active women are recommended a daily intake of 2,000 calories, while younger children, inactive women, and older adults are recommended just 1,800 calories a day. Teenage boys and active men need more —around 2,800 calories a day. Remember that we're all different—it's what makes us unique. Chances are your body shape is right for you.

*Although life is busy—school, exams, not to mention your social life—it's important to make healthy eating part of your balanced lifestyle.*

## No Time Like the Present

Your teenage years are the perfect time to start good eating habits and to take up regular exercise. In your teens, you're likely to be busier than ever with studies, friends, and hobbies to enjoy. But take time out to think about your diet and whether you're giving your body all the nutrients it needs. Get to know how your body works for you, and what you can eat and drink to get it working at its full potential. Good habits will benefit your health now, and will put you on a good, healthy path for the future.

### REAL LIFE

*"I've always been heavier than my friends. It used to upset me. I wanted to be like everyone else. My doctor told me about good eating habits and ways to exercise. I've lost some weight and am much fitter these days. But I've also come to recognize that I'm never going to be slim. My friends say it doesn't matter—it's who I am, not what I look like."*

*Amy, 14*

### TOP 10 TIPS

*The following tips are good reminders of ways to keep your diet healthy.*

1. Base meals on starchy foods and proteins.
2. Eat lots of fruits and vegetables.
3. Eat fish once or twice a month.
4. Increase your intake of fiber.
5. Cut down on saturated fat and sugar.
6. Try to eat no more than 6 g of salt a day.
7. Get active to maintain a healthy weight.
8. Drink plenty of water.
9. Don't skip breakfast.
10. Enjoy your food!

# Glossary

**adolescence** the time of development between the beginning of puberty and adulthood

**anxiety** a feeling of worry or tension

**atrophy** the partial or complete wasting away of the body

**blood pressure** the pressure of blood against the walls of blood vessels

**body mass index** a measure of how much fat your body contains

**calories** the units used to measure the amount of energy in food

**depression** an illness or emotional state of gloom and deep sadness

**diabetes** a condition in which the body does not produce, or sometimes respond to, insulin and so is unable to regulate the amount of sugar in the blood

**gene** a tiny unit of inheritance, found in DNA

**genetics** The study of genes and inheritance

**glucose** a type of sugar that your body cells convert into energy

**hormones** chemicals produced in the body that control many different processes, such as body changes during puberty

**metabolism** the amount of energy your body burns to maintain itself

**metabolize** to deal with chemicals coming into the body, using them for nutrition or respiration or getting rid of them

**obesity** when a person has an abnormally high amount of body fat, or a BMI greater than 30.0

**osteoporosis** a disease that causes bones to weaken, making them more prone to breaking

**puberty** the time at the beginning of adolescence when the sex organs mature

**secrete** to give out

**stress** an emotional feeling of strain, tension, or anxiety and a physical state of the body

**vitamin** a substance that is essential, in very small amounts, for health

# Further Information

## Books

*Keep Your Cool!: What You Should Know About Stress (Health Zone)*
by Sandra Donovan
Lerner Publications, 2009.

*Mirror Image: How Guys See Themselves (What's the Issue?)*
by Adam Woog
Compass Point Books, 2009.

*Explaining Diabetes (Explaining…)*
by Anita Loughrey
Smart Apple Media, 2010.

*Living with Obesity (Teen's Guides)*
by Nicolas Stettler
Checkmark Books, 2010.

*The Skin You're In: Staying Healthy Inside and Out (Scholastic Choices)*
by Diane Webber
Children's Press, 2008.

*Frequently Asked Questions About Athletes and Eating Disorders (FAQ: Teen Life)*
by Barbara A. Zahensky
Rosen, 2009.

## Web Sites

**American Academy of Family Physicians: The Exercise Habit**
http://familydoctor.org/online/famdocen/home/healthy/physical/basics/059.html

**Health Canada: Food and Nutrition**
http://www.hc-sc.gc.ca/hl-vs/iyh-vsv/food-aliment/index-eng.php

**Mayo Clinic: Nutrition and Healthy Eating**
http://www.mayoclinic.com/health/nutrition-and-healthy-eating/MY00431

**My Pyramid**
http://www.mypyramid.gov

**Nutrition Data: Know What You Eat**
http://www.nutritiondata.com/

**U.S. Centers for Disease Control: Calculate Your BMI**
http://www.cdc.gov/healthyweight/assessing/bmi/

**USDA: Food and Nutrition Information Center**
http://fnic.nal.usda.gov/nal_display/index.php?info_center=4&tax_level=1

**The World Health Organization**
http://www.who.int

# Index